States of Matter

Gases

by Rebecca Pettiford

Bullfrog Books

Ideas for Parents and Teachers

Bullfrog Books let children practice reading informational text at the earliest reading levels. Repetition, familiar words, and photo labels support early readers.

Before Reading
- Discuss the cover photo. What does it tell them?
- Look at the picture glossary together. Read and discuss the words.

During Reading
- "Walk" through the book with the reader. Discuss new or unfamiliar words. Sound them out together.
- Look at the photos together. Point out the photo labels.

After Reading
- Prompt the child to think more. Ask: Gas is a state of matter. Can you name any other states of matter?

Bullfrog Books are published by Jump!
5357 Penn Avenue South
Minneapolis, MN 55419
www.jumplibrary.com

Copyright © 2026 Jump! International copyright reserved in all countries. No part of this book may be reproduced in any form without written permission from the publisher.

Jump! is a division of FlutterBee Education Group.

Library of Congress Cataloging-in-Publication Data is available at www.loc.gov or upon request from the publisher.

ISBN: 979-8-89213-957-1 (hardcover)
ISBN: 979-8-89213-958-8 (paperback)
ISBN: 979-8-89213-959-5 (ebook)

Editor: Jenna Gleisner
Designer: Anna Peterson

Photo Credits: iStock, cover, 22; SpiffyJ/iStock, 1; djmilic/iStock, 3; Olena Tur/Shutterstock, 4, 6–7, 23bl; DedMityay/Shutterstock, 5, 23tm; simonkr/iStock, 8, 12–13, 23tl; wk1003mike/Shutterstock, 9; Artiom Photo/Shutterstock, 10–11; dragonsforest/Shutterstock, 14–15, 23tr; audiznam260921/Shutterstock, 16–17, 23br; ThamKC/Shutterstock, 18; banjongseal324SS/Shutterstock, 19; Altitudevs/Dreamstime, 20–21; irin-k/Shutterstock, 24.

Printed in the United States of America at Corporate Graphics in North Mankato, Minnesota.

Table of Contents

Full of Air	4
Blow Bubbles	22
Picture Glossary	23
Index	24
To Learn More	24

Full of Air

Look! A hot air balloon! It **floats**.

It is full of hot air.

Air is a **gas**.

Gas is **matter**.

It is made of **particles**.

They are far apart.

They move fast!

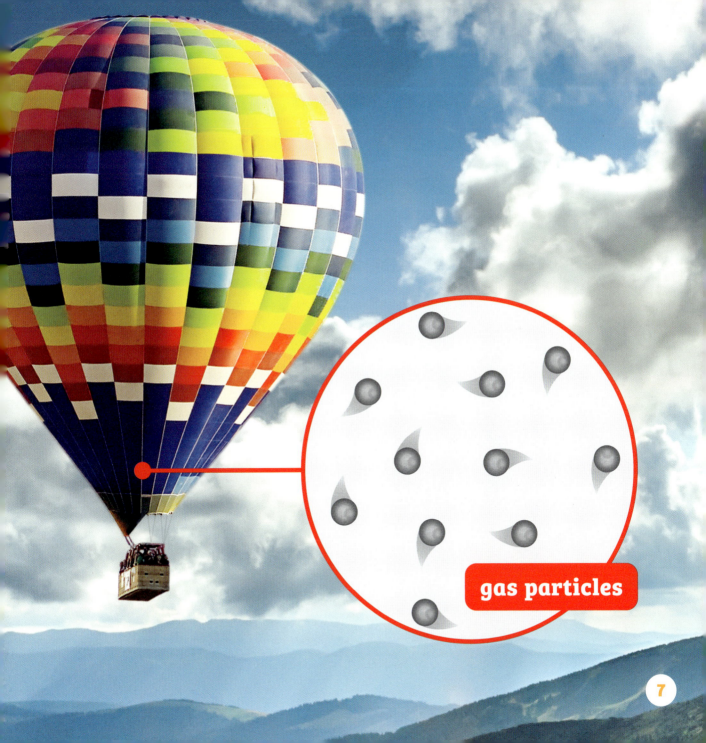

Gas takes up space.
Nick blows up a balloon.

Air fills it.

Gas has weight.

Helium is a gas.

This balloon is filled with it.

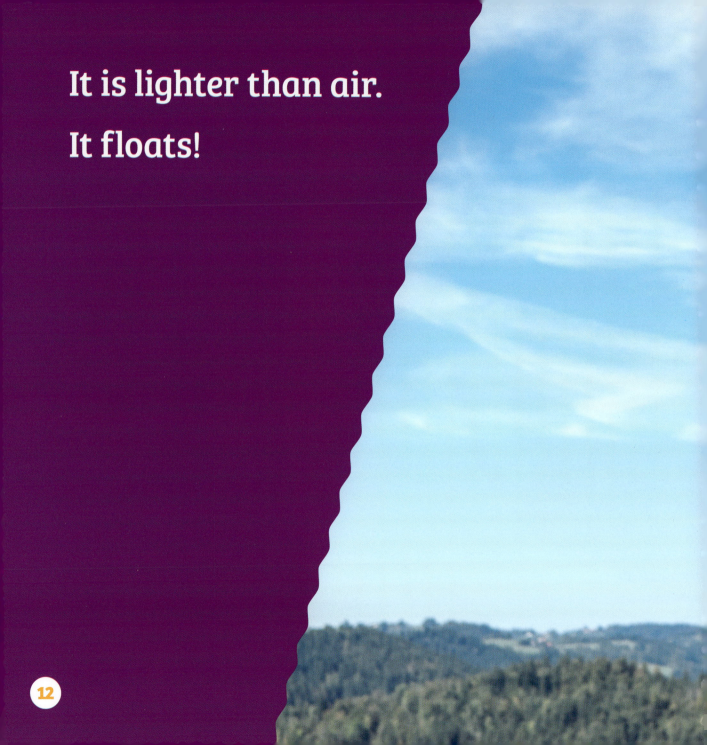

It is lighter than air.

It floats!

Gas can change.

Air cools.

It changes to **liquid**.

We see dew on grass.

Mom makes tea.
See the **steam**?
It is a gas.

Cody sips a drink.

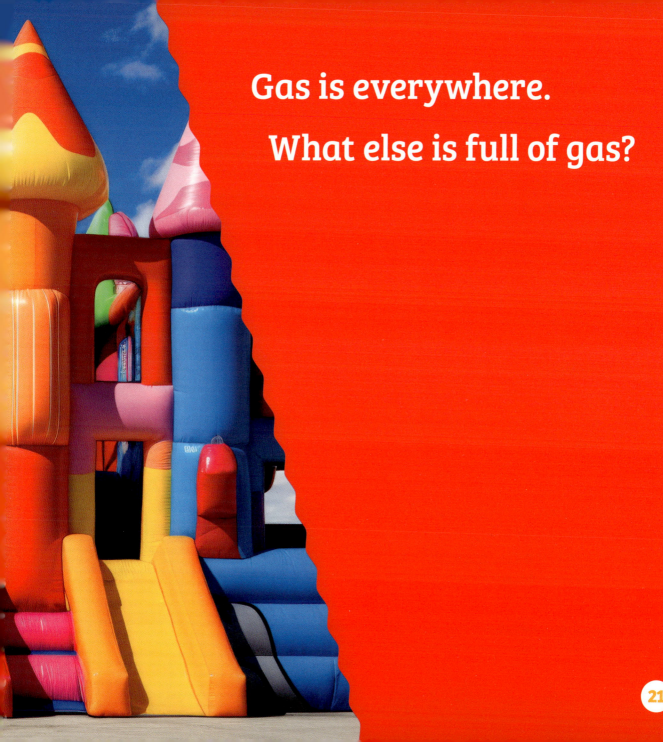

Gas is everywhere.

What else is full of gas?

Blow Bubbles

Bubbles are pockets of gas. Use your breath to make bubbles! Ask an adult for help measuring and mixing.

What You Need:
- large cup
- spoon
- bubble wand
- teaspoon
- measuring cup
- dish soap
- water
- sugar

Steps:
1. Measure a ½ cup (118 milliliters) of dish soap. Pour it into a large cup.
2. Measure 1 ½ cups (355 mL) of water. Add it to the cup.
3. Measure 2 teaspoons (10 mL) of sugar. Add it to the cup.
4. Stir with the spoon.
5. Dip the bubble wand in the mixture.
6. Blow bubbles!

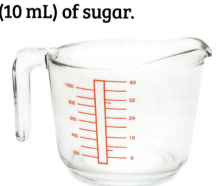

Picture Glossary

floats
Rests on top of water or hangs in the air.

gas
A state of matter that has no size or shape.

liquid
A substance that flows and can be poured.

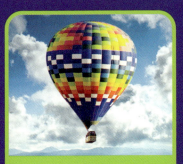

matter
Something that has weight and takes up space, such as a solid, liquid, or gas.

particles
Extremely small pieces of something.

steam
A gas that forms when water is heated to its boiling point.

23

Index

air 5, 9, 12, 15
balloon 8, 11
bubbles 19
dew 15
floats 4, 12
helium 11

hot air balloon 4
liquid 15
matter 6
particles 6
steam 16
weight 11

To Learn More

Finding more information is as easy as 1, 2, 3.

❶ Go to **www.factsurfer.com**
❷ Enter **"gases"** into the search box.
❸ Choose your book to see a list of websites.